FIRST-TIME
LISTENER

ESSENTIAL POETS SERIES 297

ONTARIO ARTS COUNCIL
CONSEIL DES ARTS DE L'ONTARIO

an Ontario government agency
un organisme du gouvernement de l'Ontario

Canada Council   Conseil des arts
for the Arts   du Canada

Guernica Editions Inc. acknowledges the support of
the Canada Council for the Arts and the Ontario Arts Council.
The Ontario Arts Council is an agency of the Government of Ontario.
We acknowledge the financial support of the Government of Canada

Jennifer Zilm

FIRST-TIME
LISTENER

GUERNICA
EDITIONS
TORONTO · CHICAGO · BUFFALO · LANCASTER (U.K.)
2022

Guernica Founder: Antonio D'Alfonso

Michael Mirolla, general editor
Anna van Valkenburg, editor
Cover and interior design: Rafael Chimicatti
Cover image: Ryan Jones & Jennifer Zilm
Guernica Editions Inc.
287 Templemead Drive, Hamilton, (ON), Canada L8W 2W4
2250 Military Road, Tonawanda, N.Y. 14150-6000 U.S.A.
www.guernicaeditions.com

Distributors:
University of Toronto Press Distribution (UTP)
5201 Dufferin Street, Toronto (ON), Canada M3H 5T8
Independent Publishers Group (IPG)
814 N Franklin Street, Chicago, IL 60610, U.S.A
Gazelle Book Services, White Cross Mills
High Town, Lancaster LA1 4XS U.K.

First edition.
Printed in Canada.

Legal Deposit – Third Quarter
Library of Congress Catalogue Card Number: 2022934697
Library and Archives Canada Cataloguing in Publication
Title: First time listener / Jennifer Zilm.
Names: Zilm, Jennifer, author.
Series: Essential poets ; 297.
Description: Series statement: Essential poets series ; 297
Identifiers: Canadiana 20220192820 | ISBN 9781771837460 (softcover)
Classification: LCC PS8649.I52 F57 2022 | DDC C811/.6—dc23

*This book is for Ryan Jones
and the holy conversation.*

Contents

2. RETROSPECTIVE OF THE NORTH IN GOLD

3. LOST TIME

"We are born voyeurs. The sense of hearing is the first we acquire and the last we lose."

—**Mary Ruefle**

"They tend to adhere to a different set of norms ... in an age of digital distraction, they connect with enthusiasm to a decidedly analog device: they listen ... for longer periods, with greater attention, and with greater loyalty than do audiences at any other time ... They tend to listen alone—alone in bed, alone on a highway, alone in the world—and find that a voice in the darkness offers a bond with a wider community. Perhaps you're one of them."

—**Timothy Lavin**

An epidemiology of recent muse-naming patterns

Workshop the fuck out of me, Muse.
Riding a triple digit bus to Howe Sound
to find an old summer camp on Keats Island,
passing a Chinese dollar store perpetually
going out of business, I lift my eyes
from the open windows on my Blackberry
to catch sight of a recycling billboard:
An afterlife for every blue.

A black eBook in my first window,
an owl purple on its cover:
Step out of your dress and into the poem.
My mentor's email, window two,
from old-city Vilnius. *I'm a muse poet,*
but money's tight so perhaps I can give you
some hints about slant rhymes and where
you might find her.

Behind window number three: a ruin
of hymned data—a dynamic red map
traces an epidemiology of daughter names.
See how Emily infects from the Northwest,
Ashley from some confederate longing
in the deep. I'm after Muse Zero.
I don't know her exact dates
but suspect she was born in the 'ember
months of '79 or the 'ary months
of 1980.

The map suggests her name is Jennifer,
Kimberley, Allison or Rebecca,
but I suspect like a hooker she has
a secret name unknown even to her mother.
With my shitty devices, in all
of God's dirty little databases,
on my city's hurt ocean roads, I sought her.
At Crab Park, thought I saw her sleeping

—that lovely girl of water and harbour,
that high modernist's imaginary daughter—
and in a suburban strip club, glimpsed her
moulting like a Russian nesting doll.
Her breath wrecked by hairspray, she kissed me
once in a bar called *Numbers*.

In Tarot class, the four of cups
warned me against rejoicing in easy loss.
The context of the query was *Queen of Cups*,
which means *mother* but also *magic*. After that,
I had peaceful nightmares, mindful
nightmares.

Over the bridge is a new suburb.
A ferry is just a bus walking on water.
On Keats Island there's no reception
and a few fields cleared for my waiting.
Once it gets dark, there will be owls
everywhere.

1.
ASK ME!

QUERY: How do I know when my iBook has ended?

ANSWER: Thank you for your query.

We are deep in the midst of making
live a website on how to keep paper
sacred with marginalia; tracking how sleep
science and bibliomancy are beginning
to map the common reader's kisses
with densitometers and infra-red light.
Please note that when your sticky fingers
tap the screen to flip the final page,
an approbation will appear: "CONGRATS!
YOU'VE JUST FINISHED A BOOK!" This is
to assure you of your accomplishment
because our designers suspect users
might get lost without weight on either side
of paragraphs. Rest assured a series of atoms
wait in stasis to bubble up to greet you.
Anyways. Back to the antique reader's kisses.
The secret to ancient books is to imagine
a road without street lamps, before
that lunatic flew his key-kite in the rain.
Pre electricity, readers slept from dusk
to midnight then opened their eyes
for a day rehearsal. A Coptic monk with his
grey-stringed beard, a girl with stringy hair
falling in bits from some somnambulant bonnet
would hit the books with candles and frankincense.

Our data set consists of wax patterns and fingernail
grit mapped to follow his preferred 2-a.m. prayer,
to unearth her favourite passage. Further,
stray hairs squished into vellum suggest the moment
(our best hypothesis is 3 a.m.) when both
returned to sleep. I suppose you might say
we cartographers of the codex try
to give new meaning to the term 'dirty books.'

**HOW SATISFACTORY
DID YOU FIND THIS REPLY?**

Journal for the Study
of the Signs of the Apocalypse

keywords: wild-fires; wind-chimes;
Oak Bay deer cull; heart-metrics

Someone in the nation of Georgia
downloaded a thesis: *Heart*
Knowledge: Towards a (W)holistic
Eco-literacy in Teacher Education.

On the island, smoke drifting
from the mainland transformed
the morning sky off-white as
a retired librarian watched
a day-dazed bat skitter its wings
past her brunch plate.

Someone in Pakistan has down-
loaded an article: *The Relational*
Narrative Desire: Inter-
Subjectivity and Trans-
Subjectivity in the Novels
of HD and Virginia Woolf.

The island capital is alarmed
with wind-chimes; late-night
buses commence their voyages
at half past six. At the corner
of Vancouver and Cook, the driver

tenderly unloads an ancient,
crippled passenger into dusk.

Someone in St. Petersburg has
downloaded a book chapter:
*Exploring Stimulant Treatment
in Technology-Enhanced Consumer
Behaviour.*

A guest in a bedroom where green
improvises on blue draped
a sheer, leopard print scarf
over the mirror; can't bear
to meet herself face-to-face.

Someone in Sweden accessed
a working paper: *Taking a Silver
Maple for a Bride: Towards a Full
Understanding of Dendrosexual Equality.*

Layering *Miracle* anti-age lotion
on my chin, I elbowed
a miniature statue of the virgin
mother out of a window,
(someone somewhere
accessed something
about *click curation*
and *24 paintings of flowers*
and *white girls*) and I waited
for full absorption before
going to retrieve her.

Devotional: Hastings & Princess

My icon-bearing wall, the paint lightfast,
refusing the sun's sleazy degradation.
Egg tempera is preferable to watercolour
because the leftover white can be used to
tighten widening pores or as scramble
for brunch after matinal devotions.
We who eat our god prefer our worship
objects with an edible sheen.
Out of the church, away from my altar, I find myself
praying to electric lights, to nostalgia,
to steam, to the gentled railway tracks,
feast of freighter colour, power of
placement, oh our sweet lady of basic
bitch variations. I drink coffee only
at cafes where beans are locally roasted,
like Joan of Arc. On a bus shelter
I saw a sign: *Someone took my brother*—
I mean—*my bicycle,* I must learn how
to identify an emergency.

QUERY: *How do I resume?*
Can I use emoji in business emails?

ANSWER: Thank you for your query.

There is a moment we all ask ourselves: When will I be able to go into the organic grocer and purchase *all-I-can-eat*-quinoa with a flash of pink nipple?

Business etiquette is indeed in flux. Sometimes, a handwritten note makes the difference with an employer; those loops and whorls, with curriculum reform, have become almost cuneiform and a way to distinguish yourself from younger aspirants. Epigraphy really is a growth industry. Here are the metrics

of the situation. Metrics means digits: write 4 not f-o-u-r. Here is a situational question. When your subordinate enters the office with her head in her hands—like a 4th century saint—how do you tactfully tell her she really needs to modernise and mobilize productivity?

Can you play productively by yourself?
Do you have the leadership skills to take your place at third base and still convey to the outfielder that she is a valued member of the team? Positive re-enforcement

is so important. When she forestalls a homerun
—1- handed—make sure she throws the softball and not her skull. Seriously, weren't you tasked with resolving this

situation 2 stanzas ago? Be sure to let her know you are very concerned with her deliverables. (O my headless ~~one~~ 1!)

HOW SATISFACTORY!

The rare books cataloguer: A day in the life

Tasked with one item per day, the rare books
    librarian—
graduate of the finest iSchool in Long Island
    —is well-versed
in standards and professional development seminars.
~~
The tip of his tongue holds the fugitive names hiding
in 34 distinct acronyms. He fancies himself now
as something like a pre-bellum European poet;

his goatee would perpetually radiate Romanticism if only
he could dwell perpetually in a sepia shard of graphic material.
    Imagine Rilke
petting his domesticated panther or tracing the gleaming

white six-pack of that guillotined god torso.
Thus, the rare books librarian in his daily appraisal:
thick, gloved fingers surveying the breakage along a spine,

a bone of jutting copper, a fin de siècle volume slightly greater
than a well-bred lady's palm. The first principle of diplomatics
states that you can assess form without apprehending content,

the cover the site of judgement after all. Still there is no simple
formula to diagnose whether a book is rare or merely second
    hand.
He examines today's waxy relief on green carefully: some sort

of amphora that stems into a woman's tapered torso,
her upraised arms holding a sprawl of leaf and stem
that he likens in his notes to the tattoo

emblazoned on the chest bone above the boat neckline
of the new community college coop girl in reception
whose hair is dreaded beneath a cowboy-red bandana.

The vase-woman is empire waisted, he notes,
but the t-shirt reads *Open Access*. No: strikethrough.
He's confused again. That's not the cover-maiden

but rather the thick-armed technician breaking his appraisal
with the swift twist of her sharpening complimentary
    HB pencils,
her cheerful frisking, seeking covert ballpoint pens from
    the bodies

of strangers. Soon she will pass him again in a waft of glycerine
and sandalwood to retrieve a box of reconsidered ephemera
or a toe-tagged first edition: he needs a question to
    convey his ken,

that ground wood pages deteriorate easily from within,
    that he knows
all the best methods of both/how to distinguish between
conservation and preservation. So he says, *how do they do
    the colour?*

Meaning of course what pigments were utilized to populate
the vines and flowers on her chest, meaning archival quality?
Her finger flicks a bright collarbone leaf, *Cadmium*, she says,
or mercury. The yellow is definitely zinc.

Water and other volatiles

At that time, I had 20k followers—
chipmunks mostly, but also robins
and probably some CIA. Monitoring
the feeders like a police scanner,
it's hard to moderate all the lives
funnelled through this interface.
I crossed over the bridge, out of the forest,
to present my research on social media
sentiment analysis. The feedback:
there will always be violence, hatred.

In the hospital, the social worker's
fingers were stained citrus, she smelled
of cologne samples, like someone
who didn't know how to give
anything away. She chirped, *We've found
you housing, We must house you, We are
ending street homelessness.* I live in a park.
She said, *Oh street contains* "park" *for
purposes of city classification.*

Classify is a synonym for *keep
secret* and it's hard to sleep
in a high-rise, after months in the forest.
I dry out, take baths, think of my lost
followers. At the follow up, I tell her
about the desiccation. She says, *Well it's
nuanced isn't it? Water is a spectrum*

disorder: dry/damp/wet. In the tub,
"how high's the water, mama?" becomes
a diagnostic question. "Looks like
we'll be blessed with a little more rain"
describes a symptom. Better volatile
than refractory, in any case.

QUERY: I have to write a paper on Gilgamesh? What is a Gilgamesh?

ANSWER: Thank you for your query.
Gilgamesh is by far the most cutting
edge piece in our line of antediluvian handbags.
Artisanal—well-*crafted* not well-*extracted*—
leathersmiths in tandem with fishers
and hookers stitched the finest polyamides
over distressed leather to form a purse
of composite nature. The inner pocket
is raw cowhide, big enough to hold
your house keys or a pill box. The exterior
is fishnet—the mesh in our gilga—
and large enough to bear just about anything
solid and waterproof: perhaps an umbrella,
I have a hunch it's really gonna pour.

As with all our products, **SATISFACTION
IS GUARANTEED!**

Postdiluvian baggage

Bob Dylan is the best in the basement.
I mean greatest hits vol. 2 on tape!
I am a child in a jump seat driving—
being driven—along another tree line
from the Isle of Vancouver to some shit-
hole logging town, when a 20-year-old
Jewish kid says *10,000 miles of grave
yard mouths,* now forever I'm a shiksa
slut who hates camping.
But side two, cheerful,
tells me *I'm riding high, going no-
where* tomorrow with my arriving bride
and big boxes along King George Hwy
—read *The Brick* and *The Rock*—
and now I'll spend my life with bible, apocalyptic,
a chip on a bare-freckled shoulder.

Bible salesman

I heard *palimpsest* my final year
in Bible College and it sounded like
something I should avoid, illegal.
Like the feds investigating
the recesses of a dusty mountain hollow.
Familiar and exotic at the same time.
So no antiquities for me.
I can stand behind a product bound
in white leatherette, illustrations:
nothing more lurid than a high-end
cookbook. Did you see the insert
where the Lord pulls the corpse
from the cave? Substitute Lazarus for
a Virginia Ham and imagine the Lord's
outer garment as an apron. Just yesterday
I told a customer: *Look Lucy! I know
a roast on Sunday is important, but
your family can't live on Spam alone!*
So professionally I like to strike
a balance—brand new luxury,
nothing crusty. In my downtime,
travelling, I make a practice of keeping
each Gideon Bible. Nights, lonely
in motel rooms, I hunger for the strange,
freely available. Yank open
my bedside table and there it is:
like having a guaranteed clean
hooker in each town. Can I get an Amen?

Hey! Fever

It's the ragweed in the winter, she sniffed.
The planet is warming, the spores float
fifteen clicks off the coast, even winter
isn't safe to breathe anymore. For years
didn't know that I was allergic, why
I cried each time I went outside. Hormones
or poetic sensibilities, maybe. A road trip
through Badlands was persuasive. Pulling off
the interstate in August for a *Scenic View*:
one thousand shades of brown, tent rocks,
a canyon. A sign beside the washrooms:
The stillness of the land is a disguise,
and I stared out through red eyes, sneezing.

QUERY: *When I archive an email where does it go?*

ANSWER: Thank you for your query.

It's important to understand your archive as your fonds. This means we like you and honour the sedimentary accrual of your correspondence. Think of each archive as a geological site. You are your own living finding aid but the cloud is the geologist, if you know what I mean. Being so fond we worry about you storming through your living room, your storage locker with a ruler measuring stacks of paper, the state of original disorder. Remember the coolest teacher in your high school; you'd swear and he'd say *keep it clean kids*, but nothing more than that.

HOW SATISFIED ARE YOU?

Spend some time with the word: *tender*

My friend who works in city housing informs me:
since I stood in the exploded body, I haven't

been sleeping right. Meaning: as in meat,
verb, to soften an animal carcass. This friend,

vocationally ½ butcher ½ care aide,
taught me the difference between the verbs:

Harvest & *forage.* I am appropriating
all of this. Meaning: a ship providing

respite/sustenance to another ship
mid-ocean. He is also my tenant.

I am at last a landlord. Meaning: currency,
an exchange of goods for services.

We have it on good authority the popular
organisational guru is really some sort

of deep agent. Her trigger word must be
TENDER, meaning: soft, delicate like

hand-folded silk neckties. We communicate
mostly over an almost obsolete platform as

I am shuttling on the train through the outer suburbs,
the minor skyscrapers a great a forest of light

meaning: *oh my baby, oh my baby, oh my*

Culmination Card: The Emperor

1.
Online gambling with pixelated Tarot cards,
the Emperor in Outcome position persuades me
that *placing trust in a father, husband, partner or
other man will come up trumps*. I lower
my sleek bundle of aluminium, glass and light,
and prone on my new sofa I observe
this long body; asleep in red t-shirt.
Three weeks in our first date is just beginning.

His profile listed his profession as *lighting technician*
and confirmed his deepest suspicions:
the moon is a total hoax. And since
the last emperor left with a text message:
(Can I borrow yr copy of *Never Let Me Go*?)
why not furl out this winter inquisition and
wait for the trees to father new blossoms?
I can bear another wet February in love
with nothing but this, the memory of petals
falling onto the still sometimes-wet pavement.
Remember that ultimately pink will rule again this city.

2.
My medium missed some things—existence
of a secret father god who hid in an aviary,
his hands holding dead bees for twelve years
of hours. The men leave; these small
slutty losses all bear the signature

of the first leaving. But now my thou,
my shining startled bright body of holes
you will not let go. Diplomat, you
present me a burnt stew of peppers,
pasta steamed with sauerkraut, so I
invite you to share my two rooms
to prove to me that you can cook.

You will be able to know if you can trust
your emperor if you sleep well together.
He will throw out his meth pipe and serve you
minestrone soup abundant with raw garlic,
a garnish of magnesium tablets and
transparent gold capsules of salmon oil
to form a still life for your Insta when it catches
the venetian blind-slated light. O my beloved

is to me as a montage of carefully curated
archival news footage.

QUERY: *How big is the data?*
Can I compress losslessly?

ANSWER: Thank you for your query.

Not sorry. Big data is essentially an accounting of nouns in a 21st century poem. Think of nouns as the nerves of the sonnet. At this point we are focusing on outwitting decay, preserving our syntactic heritage. Once, in primary school, we toured Dairy Queen and they allowed us into a locked freezer, a whole room of ice. Unfortunately, cold storage only forestalls archival erosion. Ice cream or emails, the artefact won't last forever. We risk getting sticky to chart the metrics of our collection. Now, more than ever, the mindful mining of values is crucial. Our accountants of lights are soft-penciling through wrecks of texts to present an account to the disinterested public. Our deliverable will be a frilled list of people, places, things. Please pay attention before rust erodes the pronouns and the aubade seems equivocal. Of the degradation of morning we are certain.

ARE YOU SATISFIED?

Crimes of the century: A CNN interpretation

> *"If not now, when?*
> the fanatic asks.
> *If not me*, the president says, *then who*?"
> —*American Fanatics*
> Dorothy Barresi

i. Drowning

Here is a live stream, illegal, surreal.
Here is a flood, a submerge, a nine-one-
one call: *Do you need fire? Ambulance?*
Police? I need you to send someone. One
daughter, four sons in the master, another
in the tub face up: *Quiver-full,*
the cop says, *it made me shake. All water*
and I thought it was a doll: the daughter.
Jury foreman says: "*godly women*
know better than to trust what Satan says."
Her husband worshipped God, worked for NASA,
becomes lawyer, remarries. Defense says:

I have long since crossed the boundary, she
is daughter to me now, she is daughter.

ii. Exchange student

Young! Beautiful! Trouble! Ugly American
on steroids. Something in her eyes suggests
she was high and hooking in amongst
the limestone buildings brimming with art and altars.
Once you read Italian, headlines are all
gangland, drug crime in epic cycle.
The accused was good with languages,
living with an off-beat Etruscan
and a lass—British and thus more elegant.
How many people fall in love at twenty-
three and think forever? It was All Saints'
Day and, I hate to say, this was just

garden variety: one guy kills one girl.
Nevertheless, the papers went crazy.

iii. Assassination attempt

Rawhide, really, is the best code name.
I thought it was fireworks! the president
recalls, *a handful of bright red frothing,*
did I just bite my tongue? So we went to
the trauma centre, though it had nothing
by way of security. *Today we*
are all Republicans, the Dr. said,
as he shifted the heart to one side, held
its beating in his latex hand. Dutch was
in character the entire time. He said,
the assassin—attempted—I wish him
no harm. The crawl at the bottom in white:

HE SAYS HE HAD NO DIRECTION IN LIFE.
Note: all caps; note: Condensed Helvetica.

iv. Oklahoma

The impact, the shockwave, like an iceberg,
hit downtown at the destination point
of the trail of tears. Was it a whack-job?
A professional? You don't have to be
a rocket scientist to build a bomb.
The smoke cleared like T-zone trouble with
a bit of astringent. Here a Survivor
of the Journal Record Bureau, here a
Survivor of the Social Security
Office. The bomber slept in a motel
called Dreamland. *Turns out he was one of ours;
therefore we needed to know who he was.*

Voted most talkative, his childhood marked
by one hateful novel, then nine stories.

v. The Branch

The agent's story is backed by the Chair
of the Centre for the Study of Hate.
There are only two research questions:
*I had a guy on the line who thought he was
God* and *it was a situation of
biblical proportions.* Think cubits. Think
shekels. Somehow the church became cult, the raid
a debacle. The Dallas affiliate
has God live via satellite. *Sir, may
I ask how you are doing? Ah,* God answers,
*fair to middlin' but I am weakening.
The power's intermittent but sometimes*

they bombard us with noise and light. So calm,
you can't help but begin to wonder.

Politics

The attorney general spends his grief
in after-dinner books: poetry, Hebrew
Bible and Aeschylus; annotates
his longing in the gutters. Blue eyes
read the ocular wheels of the chariot:
the fixed pupils, the eye all gone
true black, a brother's brain in mid-
line shift. He dictates a note to his wife
through his manservant: *Hon, I am*
skipping breakfast. I'll be down here
in the dizzy writing letters to our
daughter—the unborn or the one
upstairs. Just make sure one of them
gets it.

begotten.com

The first book you open on New Year's Day turns
your thoughts to Texas and criminal
justice. *Cooling Time,* you think, a respite
from volumes dense with white space and serif stanzas.
Instead, watch a stream of *Friday Night Lights*
first thing in the morning. WebMD confirms:
medically you are still young but past
a trilogy of decades, a small collection
of your very own dead draws you
to public library terminals; to stare
at dissected, digitized pages: a yearbook,
a landing document, a log from a ship
harboured in Hawaii, an online entry
in the Itawamba County Book of the Dead.
All the wars of your charismatic hillbilly grandfathers.
O how much of your prenatal past can you gather
with targeted search terms and the baptizing efforts
of the Latter Day Saints! Ancestry.com has rooted
your inexplicable heart to the Fat Elvis
and your platonic love for states so humid
they'd leave you wrecked and spinstered at 30.
Be warned: There were few plantations this far west|
and some Union sympathy, it's possible
your forefather may have fought for the Other
side. Migration: it's not just
for data anymore. West to Texas
where the census ticks them off as farmers
and notes a girl child, her family name

different from the head of the household.
Then North to the border, Washington,
a great-grandma cooking, a great-grandpa teaching
music. Their son takes a foreign bride,
flees to Alaska, stateless, to spawn blonde children
for black and white photos, half hiding behind
placards proclaiming *WE LIKE IKE*. Oh, look away.
It's a lie, the grins too toothy to be anything
but terrified. *Boom* up from the basement,
almost as soon as the territory is incorporated;
scatter the progeny from even the memory of hot lands
to a bankrupt, gold rush province only recently
confederated. A rainy place, no union, just lost
paternity and you—a medically young girl child,
four family names removed, seeking through a screen
what it is to be begotten.

QUERY: *Is it true I can get any book online?*

ANSWER: Thank you for query.
Apologies. It turns out that the Alexandrian library
was mostly magical thinking on our parts. All our parts.
The process of culling books from a library is called
weeding. We believe that our colleagues
in Alexandria started innocently in the Dewey decimal.
In the 800s, they noted low circ numbers and
the incoming rush of papyrus. Of the making of many books.
Panicking, looking at shelf space. Like all good gardeners,
they pulled & yanked & composted. They recycled.
Have you experienced the easy, satisfying drag
& click of an icon from your desktop?
The simulated crackle of emptying? Imagine Egypt
& those non-unionized book workers lugging
unread tomes to the corner. Feel the tightening
& lengthening of their shoulder muscles.
Visualize spring & remember your own cleaning.
Forgive their zeal. They trusted—as I know you do
—that the materials would be repurposed:
that out of sight doesn't mean out of mind.
Those books are somewhere, seriously.
If it's hard to locate stuff in the wisps & binary pollution
of the cloud, imagine pawing through the back alleys
& steel bins of an Alexandrian summer. In the end,
we must all learn to trust the good folks
in waste management. Leave it to the experts.
In the end, nothing is really discarded.

SATISFIED?

2.
RETROSPECTIVE
OF THE NORTH IN GOLD

Retrospective of the North in gold

I began this poem wondering
about the quality of light pulled
past Rembrandt's spiral staircase, over
those Calvinist milkmaids, then into
Van Gogh's spasm of wheat and sunflowers.

I had just returned from the hardware store
where a handwritten sign said, *Please!*
Only three swatches per customer.
A white-trash Cassandra, I closed my eyes
and drew from the *Golden Fields* Collection:

Sundress, Candleglow, Honey Bee. In my apartment
just before twilight, the eggy surfaces of the icon corner
caught the sun from my one west-facing window:

                    an encyclopaedia of yellows.

Madonna tilts haloed headdress towards
her ginger infant and his grasping hands.
She is from Russia, a lightfast bargain purchased
from the only Orthodox supply store
in downtown Amsterdam.

Anthony, the desert's first 4th century father,
is perfect posture and shaggy, pale beard.
The monk in his cell, as painted by my significant
other behind the Japanese screen I bought in Chinatown

to bracket the book clutter, stringed instruments,
assorted inks and pigments from the rest
of the tiny living room. I wanted to capture
something about Dutch masters and
two-dimensional yellow space

                            that calls forth *ochre*,

the name of your half-breed golden retriever.
You hunched at the easel surrounded by watercolours
and oils, gently colonizing the dining hutch.
I was not your daughter

     but could have been: you were huge
and Dutch and chose the North for its light,
the Skeena in late winter; though it never
appeared to me as it did on your canvas;
though perhaps it's just not possible

to admit the influence of pink on rivers, at 12,
wearing black denim. Wealthy with blonde daughters,
you gave to *Ducks Unlimited* with reservation,
wary of societies that preserve species to kill them.

From your basement I stole a photo.
Black and white, your wife holding
a steelhead by its gills on the kitchen floor
of your house in Charlotte City.

The North is a small pressure in me. A sense
memory of snow, even when it is raining.
In both testaments, it is written: *prepare
the way in the desert, make straight a path
in the wilderness.* I like the suggestion

of bare feet on slightly warm sand; but
my gut clenches when I remember every snaking
road out of the suburbs, the makeshift crosses
marking highway from Prince Rupert to Terrace
along a river whose name I have forgotten.

      I read somewhere we come out of a deep forest
of years into a valley called loneliness. Yet, I find myself
in a perpetual evergreen forest, minnows frozen
beneath my plastic boots; and my child mind visiting
bright deserts, gardens of ochre.

Lines for the flat earth fall

Twice named, the season
is here again in interludes
of wet on granite, then cloudless
sky. *Sky blue,* you said to me
in the midst of eye contact.
But the sky is so changeable,
a blue that means almost
anything. Walking back
from Third Beach we
paused by the pond.
I pulled out my phone
to snap the moon, white
between a bare branch
a gloaming sky warping
faster than I could spell
cerulean, lilac, indigo.

Whatever conspiracy
you follow, the moon
is here to make trouble
for us, you said. I
perched on a cedar stump
angling my touch screen
for the clearest angle.
The sky—the same colour
as my eyes—is also a screen,
the moon a projection.

The screen began its raining
and we walked away from
the forest, the fake moon
the flat earth, noted no curvature.

Vancouvering

If only someone had catalogued the West End
rooms we lingered in before we knew each other.
The studio apartments are obsolete, skyline
a museum of windows, gloaming's pink container.

The summer ephemeral, splattered with rainsplaining.
Think about it. Threshold seasons name themselves
with verbs. Each year, spring slightly earlier,
renovicting winter. *Clean lines,* the designers say.
Love or *List*, but I want to count the ways

neighbourhoods change their names
faster than you do.   *New East Crackton*
became *Railtown* before I realized
we'd stopped snorting coke. I sometimes
doubt that the cluttered stanzas we inhabited
ever existed.   It was easy to forget

to pay for the SkyTrain with no ticket
-taker, but now we find new ways
to thwart the turnstiles. Arms linked,
we pay one fare so we can ride together.
Busing the road deep east, down Cordova;

yesterday a stranger beside me completing
her dialectical behaviour therapy homework,
today a boy in all black reading *The Secret Agent*,
the chapter heading "East Meets West"—but he got off
before Main Street. You say the city is best

seen in alleys. Discarded bricks, rotting softwood,
bubblegum fiberglass—you salvage materials
to build a miniature house as memorial
to all the rooms that may never have existed
in time before we knew each other.

Toronto—A New York poem

FOR ORI

Geez! I said to you on Google Chat,
you sound like some Ellis Island refugee
with a name like Zakowski and a dream
of colonizing Green Point with your homemade
laptop, four windows open, simultaneously
emailing Noam Chomsky, remotely debugging
my software and IM'ing me about how Ashbery
is the only poet who gets it. I was trying
to convince you to stay in Forest Hills,
in that two-bedroom apartment,
with your *Abba* and his endless J-Dates;
and Simona Sivkoffa, your Bulgarian girlfriend
who grew up spoiled behind the Iron Curtain
before it fell in 1989. She moved to Bavaria
where everyone looked at her crossly because
she was a Slav who clearly had some Turkish blood
in her. You said Toronto was a big blank nothing;
but New York was possibility, joy and a joyfully obese
ticket agent dancing in her Metro ticketing booth.
How many Torontonians does it take to swap a light bulb?
One to change the light bulb and 4 million
to declare it a world-class event. Still, I tried for months
to convince you to apply to the Ontario Institute
for the Study of Education; but it was a lost cause because
New York City is the New Jerusalem for 21st century Jews,

you said, booking dinner dates and offering pro-bono Hebrew
translations to Norman Finkelstein.

To prove you wrong, I went to NYC for Xmas,
using my bf's dad's Marriott points
to stay in a hotel in Secaucus, riding the commuter bus
through the Holland tunnel to make pilgrimage
to the building where John Lennon was shot,
the Dakota—the same colour as a Badland Canyon.
At the Strawberry Field memorial, someone
had left a white teddy bear holding an American flag
and wearing a t-shirt that read *Just Do It!*
My footwear impractical, I searched a Kmart
in the East Village for a pair of tennis shoes
before heading back through the tunnel to stand
at my hotel window and watch the Wal-Mart parking lot:
hordes of well-meaning people with oversized shopping carts
filled with two to three new TVs on Christmas Eve, 2007.

I hated New York City and told you so. But you left anyway,
my only friend in Toronto who'd known me in Vancouver;
also, Columbia Teachers' College was a joke,
and you knew I was going to Jerusalem to study
modern Hebrew with nothing to prepare me but a bunch
of Evangelical Bible scholars. You told me to look up
your brother in Tel Aviv, but I was too shy, and instead
        drank Perfect
Vodka in my air-conditioned room in the gated student village,
watching pirated episodes of *Six Feet Under* and going nuts.
The last I saw you was that fall in Toronto when we practiced
conversational Hebrew in the Indian restaurant you loved

on Bloor Street, across from the Indian restaurant I loved
on Bloor Street because the vindaloo made me weep,
     and four blocks
east of the Indian restaurant my ginger poet friend loved
on Bloor Street because they knew all her allergies.
You asked in Hebrew, *why do you keep using the present tense?*
Then told me you saw Ashbery near the Seinfeld diner
by a mailbox, withered, ancient, and who knows what
     he was posting.

I was barely listening because my brain was broken;
and, embarrassed to admit it, I was a failed Torontonian,
planning my escape back to the post-Olympic granola
     avenues of Vancouver.
After dinner, we TTC'ed east to the Danforth —you
     always knew
where to get the best pastries—and at a table among friends
sat a blonde, face-lifted woman about the age of your
     mother speaking
as much English as she could muster before slipping
     back into Hebrew,
saying, *I LOVE I LOVE I LOVE ha sipporim ha eleh.*
And I knew, from my six weeks in the holy city, the
     last part meant *these stories.*
Also, that your name means *my light;* that Yiddish
is a hybrid of German phonemes and Aramaic characters;
and after that everything goes English again.

Crépuscule: Basic bitch variations

1. *L'heure bleue*

*The sky is different
here*, you said,
basic bitch awe
unchecked,
& you meant,
I think, violet
seen first on
particle board
reproductions
in our separate
suburban childhoods.

You meant nautical
borders between
North Shore and City—
the valley and City
never reflected a light
that compels us to speak
of gloaming with a word
that reminds us of breakfast
(crepuscular).

2. *summer vacation*

I read the first four paperback
volumes of *À la recherche du temps perdu*
in translation, "on the Island," as we call it,
as though there were only one.

On breaks from a summer job archiving open access
    articles
and trashing oligarchies in scholarly publishing:
the *Journal of Collateral Adjectives* is such a steep
    subscription.

On my back, beneath a silver maple, I finally made
my peace with trees. Thursday evenings, I'd perch
by the life vests on the ferry, accepting
the fact of islands whose names I'll never know.

In September, I slogged through *The Captive*,
The Fugitive and *Time Regained* on the sound stage
of our city. Distracted by a standing passenger
in what we now call middle age, who mumbled
as we passed light industry and far eastern SROs,

that he'd read the comic book version.
The incident of the metal ends, I misheard him,
trying to remember the name of a lovecore band,
palm sweat slickening the steel handrail,
drip dampening the pages of my open book.

3. *Windfall Persimmon Lattes*

      In the station of the Metro
there were many flights
of stairs and no elevators.
Please offer seats to war veterans,
the crippled & passengers
over the age of 75.

      Enormous, you betrayed
our West Coast affiliation;
up-talking your French,
so merchants answered in English;
alienating our elderly neighbour
when you addressed her as *tu.*

      You took the stairs
2-by-2. Navigating stations
like a civil war general:
you saw a piece of ground and knew
how to use it. Stalking through
Christmas markets & museums
while I paused to block
flashes in front of water lilies.

You bought nothing
in gift shops; but in gardens
of historic sanitariums,
you taught me slow walking
and how to forage.
The tops of fruit trees

just inches from your fingers,
you refused to pluck
a single persimmon, salvaging
in the grass for one burst
open. You held out a long
piano-playing ghoul
hand, giving me a chunk
of souvenir windfall.

First forays towards fieldwork in colour

There is always the promise
of men's knowledge. How to not
get one pregnant. A secrecy:
don't tell anyone. Sometimes red
suspenders, a button-fly
loosed, one's new almost-
breasts maybe purple. Also
a four-inch blue vein
written out from the hollow
to the edge of pale nipple.
One's mouth is painted
Toast of New York. Oh
the spectrum. It is easier to say
bleu when one cannot
distinguish between
cerulean and indigo, *rose*
as shorthand for every pink.
I say OK. Allow
the pop of snaps at the crotch
of body suit, slip of panties
to the hang of ankle. A laying
of a white play-off towel
on plaid bedspread. A pushing in.

Ornithology

1.

On the wall in my bedroom, I placed a photograph of a
desolate chair—wide-backed and wheeled. A souvenir
of an abandoned Belgian asylum, a chamber greened by
light, four windows exposing dried leaves on a concrete
floor. Then I excised two emerald birds (one ruby throated)
from a calendar long expired, and pinned their wings with
thumbtacks into the frame. The didactic labels (adolescent
male, adult female etc.) snipped by my scissors—I have no
mind for science—have been christened as Belgian asylum
birds. Known for their vibrant, illustrated feathers, their
matte habitats.

My workday shifts are alive with fauna. Plumbers,
pharmacists, workers outreaching into this strange gerund
called housing. My office is glassed on two sides for stranger
and med reception. And now she has come, my client with
fantastic black curls and her manic methadoned eyes, with
a fraction of murder in her hands. A fledgling crow fallen
onto Carrall Street from the top of a red neon retro sign
installed pre-Olympia for character. *He's been trying to fly
for days from the pavement,* a red thumb nail grazing a
feathered head, beak closed between her index and middle
fingers, *he just needs rest.* Over the phone the Urban Wildlife
Rescue protection specialist tells me: *Whatever you do,
don't allow human hands to touch it.*

My client in her upstairs room has descended gauzy swaths of perforated turquoise over her centre-justified, single bed. The Artisanal Neon Vancouver Infant Crow resting in a plastic, yellow milk crate, placed in a sag of mattress. *If you leave him in the back alley*, I tell her, *he'll probably just fly away eventually.*

Flat earth in colour: An anti ghazal

Candle glow masquerades as yellow at night.
The pink lampshade casts a glow in our bedroom.

With my index finger, I fish a blueberry from my cervix,
wet with yeast. We drink green supplements.

By the headboard: Rider Whyte's High Priestess cloaked
in blue, the letters B and J inscribed on pillars.

A suspected fistula: a connection between two hollow spaces.
You explain the difference between hues & values.

At 4 a.m., you Ombre my mouth with Scandalous™ eyeliner,
apply Julianne's red velvet lipstick. *I wish you could see yourself.*

Lancôme matte shade 457: **Plum Show**. The perfect shade
beneath the bathroom sink. I perform for you.

Listening to a flat earth podcast: *Have you ever heard anything
as ludicrous as* 'speed of light' *or* 'dark matter'?

Label my eyes *sky-blue*, sky-so-fickle. Forecast whether
indigo or turquoise will highlight the lid of our firmament.

Your hometown's frozen white snow hides a virtual desert.
My heels boots lack traction, yield with a soft crunch.

Christmas: a culpa constructed pine, purple daisies,
babies' breath, green tissue. I diaper stems in damp paper,

Caring for a cut flower is the same procedure regardless
of the blossom's occasion. I trim edges, a bouquet in my backpack.

I begin to track my cycle. You insist the moon is a deep fake,
forecast my period precisely: my wet eyes a symptom.

To know someone suddenly, utterly. Utter *baby,* empty into me.
My throat overwhelmed; your body's patterns, a place familiar.

The live stream says there is still radiation lurking
in the reindeer's lichen. *Apocalypse Porn*, you say.

How like a fawn I feel—freckled, doubting everything
I've heard about the sun, my eyes wide from stimulants.

Re: the Apollo astronauts. If you saw the creator's handiwork
up close, would you ever swear on anything again?

You say, *there you go baby*, confusing your verbs, pronouns—
you mean let's come together. We arrive when I am on top.

Is the moon beyond the barrier or merely a well-rendered image?
A projection? I can see it from our bedroom window.

Like an astral body glowing pale, I rise dizzy, gasp air;
you wipe traces of my menses from my chin with bleach.

Antibiotic equals antilife. After the IV, the scars of boils
fading soft violet beneath welts left by your long fingers.

First-time listener: A how-to guide

1.

Long-time caller, how long
before you uncover that the secret
to prayer is to shut the fuck up?

Just fold your torso forward
in child's pose before any ersatz
altar in the evening, recall the huddle

of fog nested between the sugar
refinery and the downtown bank towers
in the morning twilight from
your favourite living room window.

2.

Go deep, slowly
against all your addiction,
to speed and years of clerical
training. Speaking in
tongues, lingual
stretch from the base
to the soft head. Sometimes,
your joy really will be the same
as a certain even number of North
African ruminants: shocked,
unmoving at dawn.

3.

As preparation, make your hair
more auburn than God intended,
curl into frame against a quilt
imitating an Austrian fin de siècle
painting with variegated chunks of gold.

4.

Long-time caller, now at last I am
a first-time listener. This early
Sunday morning, I know
that each orifice will open, can
hear. O mouth's tympanic cavity,
cunt's echo chamber, asshole's
subtle vertigo. Jesus said:
He who can listen, unfold
your freakin' ears.

3.
LOST TIME[1]

The first edition of a work would have been more precious in my eyes than any other, but by this term I should have understood the edition in which I read it for the first time ... even though I am no longer the "I" who first beheld it, even though I must make way for the "I" that I then was if that "I" summons the thing that it once knew and that the "I" of today does not know.

—*Time Regained*,
Marcel Proust

---

1 To participate in the reading of a very long book is something you do alone but also simultaneously, asynchronously. By distance learning. The first time I saw a volume of the translation of *À la recherche du temps perdu*, I was 13 years old in the Surrey Public Library. At that time the title was translated as *In Remembrance of Things Past* and the volume available was vol. 4 euphemistically translated as *The cities on the Plain*. My mother told me that it was the longest novel ever written. Length and translation both conveyed importance to me then so I borrowed the book but didn't read it. 30 years later, an Albertine figure in my own life purchased a paperback copy of *Swann's Way* from a yard sale in East Vancouver. By then the translation had been rechristened as *In Search of Lost Time*. I read somewhere that the verb *rechercher* in French has both the sense of searching—in the simple sense of seeking a lost item—and researching, in the sense of systematically examining. *Remembrance* has the sense—to me at least—of re-membering, that is of reattaching parts that have fallen off of a whole (the sonic resonance of *brance* with *branch* also recalls this—as though grafting tree branches back onto a tree trunk) or including someone back into a family or club from which their membership has lapsed. *Mem* also recalls the 13th letter of the Hebrew alphabet as well as the English noun *mom* (informal form of *mother*).

i. Trigger warnings /
'somewhere outside the realm'

This fluster of leaves blackmails one:
past a walk-in closet of green.
The silver maple knows one's type,
can spot a girl who plays through
her panties, arrays herself in Eve's
original dress. The truth is the dare.
Either and Or.[2]
One finds in a gallery,
on the last day of an exhibit,
a holiday Monday in May.
A room. Set off from on-loan
superstars of post-Impressionism,
one finds paintings permanently held,
a frame holding a square familiar.
A word heard once is heard everywhere.
There are myriad ways to talk
about twilight. This room, this painting
intimist, so the internet educates.
A glow of great buildings
made small, a stub of something
one might remember.

---

2 The city of Surrey—home of the girl as punch line—is on the south bank
of the Fraser River in Metro Vancouver. The city designation is relatively new.
To say you are a Surrey Girl is to participate in a rich and dense tragi-comic
tradition.

Parks loom large. One gradually
accustoms to touch screens. One may
accidentally be encouraged
to look up by the command
compliment the sky. An early spring
tweet, unadorned, *sans* hash.
Everyone who chances to flicker
may choose to heed, and drop
handheld device, and face
upward. One might say, *Oh
pretty,* to the oaks unleafed,
the ceiling, the sky.

ii. 'one hears nothing
when one listens for the first time'[3]

Imagine God makes mix tapes,
all one's playlists. The way *Canon in D
Minor* floats upward from the studio
in one's grandfather's basement.
Splice a remix of *Old Time Religion*
or segue into *Will the Circle
Be Unbroken.* One pronounces
segue as SEEG until corrected at 24.

Fugue: One asks a healthcare professional
which came first: the state
or the music. He will admit
the music. That flight,
that fleeing. Hiding
the bottom half of a face
with a scarf. *He has
charges.*

There is no immersion
in one's elementary
education, but occasional
units concern *l'hiver*

---

3 "But often one hears nothing when one listens for the first time to a piece
of music that is at all complicated ... For our memory, relatively to the com-
plexity of the impressions which it has to face while we are listening, is infini-
tesimal" —*From a Budding Grove.*

taught through images
of Styrofoam snow. An ice hut.
Springtime in March.
It has rained today and will
tomorrow. For half an hour
a week, the immersion teacher
is on loan. Time enough just to
replace all the vowels in song,
pomme et banane, and bring items
to illustrate the other
language that already lives
in one's own home. *Déli Cinq. Flocons
de Maïs. Savon.*
One chooses to study the Bible,
because why not?
It's shorter than Proust.[4]
The message of the novel
is that the present holds
the past, just as the sweaty
lamé-suited singer at the Casino
still contains the beta-male-mama's-boy-
truck-driver who only barely
knew the power of his own hips.
O Orphée.

---

4 Marcel Proust was a novelist from France. Often it is said that his novel was
monumental. The child protagonist of Marcel Proust's novel spends much of
his early life in the fictional town of Combray. An essayist once remarked that
Newark was the great male novelist Philip Roth's Combray. By extension, Com-
bray is Marcel's Newark. Surrey is something to me indeed.

iii. Sodom suburban

In a sprawl, there is no down-
town, but closest will be
near the royally named highway.
The skyline unbroken; a motel
named the Flamingo houses
strippers, but—young—one doesn't know
and assumes the castle curves–
pink stucco as signifiers of architectural
class. Two blocks west,
the thin white of a church
with a blue onion dome.
Not entering, one knows nothing
of icons, of Byzantine eyes.

A creek runs through projects.
One learns to climb over wire fences
to evade the super. The creek is paved over
and the name of the project
remains the same. *Vert Rive.*[5]
It sounds more implausible
on the playground: *My father has
a mountain in his backyard.*
There are three sleeps until one

---

5 In terms of geographical space, the "city" of Surrey is vast. Built for cars, many of its denizens lack driver's licences or vehicles, for various economic and legal reasons, and this is possibly a contributing factor to the high auto theft rate. In the fateful year of 2001, Surrey was proclaimed the auto-theft capital of North America.

is finished with a paternal visit
and may return to one's home sprawl.
Sleeps are a unit of time.
One's childhood walled garden.
A slab of concrete and rectangle patch of soil.
One's mother planting privacy corn
to shield subsidized dirt from
the eyes of unemployed neighbours.[6]
Two buses then ocean, a day trip
within the sprawl. *Gauche*, one
should avoid mention of sand
in bathing suits. Not swimming,
knowing to move slowly
into the cold.

---

6 The length of Proust's novel is such that we are permitted to witness a society's changes with respect to light and motion. Much has been written, I suspect, about the invention of the grid, about the switch from manually-lit gas lamps to electric streetlights. In Paris, the first of these lights were installed in 1878 to commemorate the Paris Universal Exposition. In 1881, the major boulevards were all outfitted to coincide with the Paris International Exposition of Electricity. Research is underway about how this altered circadian rhythm and changed the experience of twilight. As for motion, the switch from horses to engines is worth mentioning. In vol. 1 of Proust's novel *Du côté de chez Swann* (aka *Swann's Way/ The Way by Swann/ Swann's Coast*) we see the characters (whose names I can write but not pronounce, at least not without blushing) disembarking from horse-drawn carriages. Later—as early as vol. 2 *From a Budding Grove*—the narrator employs a chauffeur to drive his motor car (and for other purposes). Wanting to make a point about this, I just typed the words "Proust, autos" into my Chromium search bar. I was directed to proustauto.com, a junkyard located in Le Haillan, a suburb of Bordeaux. Proust Autos currently has a user rate of 2.4. I don't know how they can destroy cars better; how Proust Autos can reach for those elusive five stars (cinq étoiles)? Regardless, I am triggered to recall the various degrees of legality of the "chop shops" of my Surrey youth. All the hidden commerce in rented garages, where meth was doled out as currency to young men who would dutifully, diligently dissect stolen cars.

iv. 'possible transformations during later childhood'[7]

If not books or divination, dolls also suffice.
How to cut along lines or punch out.
Adorn the dresses, layer. If porcelain,
smashing is the equivalent of ripping.[8]
How the scarcity of men
in a neighbourhood of mothers
is mirrored in collections of hard plastic.
One learns to make do, discovers
the happy Sapphic world of Barbies.
One's sister has an oral fixation:
her thumb and forefinger, Ken's feet
chewed to white plastic bone.

It is exciting to bleed, encouraged
by novels. Like having a secret,
participating with movie misfits
and American children who pray.
One's grandmother studied nursing,
so minor opioids are an acceptable
home remedy.[9]

---

7   "[I]n order to recognize any of them individually, one must resort to deduction, try to imagine the whole range of their possible transformations during later childhood."—*In the Shadow of Young Girls in Flower.*

8   The Surrey Girl is likely a regional variation of a mythic archetype. Wiktionary has it simply: "stereotype of a young woman from Surrey, British Columbia, characterised as unintelligent and promiscuous." We are to see also Essex Girls for the British variation; refer to Jersey Girls for the American.

9   To these variations, thinking of Proust, I would like to add Balbec Girls (la

Far away, an empire breaks apart
and initials represent a new reading
practice. *Unified Sustained
Silent Reading.* This is the closest
one comes to spiritual instruction,
meditation, mindful in a room
with 30 others and a supervisor.

The old branch by the bus exchange
is converted to a police station. Who
will tell one what books to read?
At some point, each thrift store ceases
to exist. One learns to take advantage
of opportunities, the holy spirit paperback.
It is embarrassing to return plastic bottles but also
a skill. An empty two-litre yields thirty cents,
a quarter exchanged for a novel
one is too young to read. See here
one's first accent aigu, think all
saints must be fictional characters.
One wants to beatify.[10]

---

demoiselle de Balbec; Les demoiselles de Balbec, the Balbec girls). Towards
the end of *In the Shadow of Young Girls in Flower* (aka *From a Budding Grove*),
the narrator spies four girls, brazenly taking the beach, one of them on a bi-
cycle. The girls are overwhelming, shocking, cocky, one of them hops over a
wealthy middle-aged sunbather when he blocks her way. The girls—rendered
in the Moncreiff translation as "the little band" (which suggests both music
and thievery)—are all distinct, but it is impossible to tell them apart, at least at
first, they are blur of sun-flushed cheeks and "hard, obstinate, mocking eyes."
The enchanted narrator speculates that they are lower class, that they must
be the girlfriends of motorcycle racers. I take this to be an idiomatic way of
saying that they are easy.

10 A punch line is the verbal realisation of a joke. The person who creates
the space for this realization is called "a straight man." Therefore, the verbal

Further out from the city gets Fundamental.
Find even halls filled with philological
lectures. Attending movies with subtitles,
one thinks glossolalia. Any way one looks at it,
one is always talking in tongues.[11]
One pays attention to the first
accent spoken by someone.
But taller, elusive, Eastern
European. One is forever mistaking
accents for French.
First dates: learn how to
break into fruit warehouses,
forage for frozen strawberries;
jimmy windows to enter houses, vacant
holding properties, on
market. How to sleep
on the floor; pull hard
on an exterior door
of an apartment building
to hide overnight in hallways.

---

set up of a joke must be "a straight line" and the realizer of the "punch line" might be "a punch man", or, to create a gender balance, "a punch girl." This places "punch" and "straight" as complements, which seems odd at first listen but we must go along. Here are four straight lines where the Surrey Girl functions as that realisation. What is the difference between a Surrey Girl and her mother? What is the difference between a Surrey Girl and a dryer? What is the difference between a Surrey Girl and a man? What is the difference between a Surrey Girl and a puppet?

11 Jokes like this are, among other things, an education in making associations, similes. The straight lines force us to first ask "how are they the same?" and thus to create an essential unity between two unlike things. (Punch lines: a. ten bucks b. a dryer doesn't follow you around for a week after you've dropped your load in it c. a Surrey Girl has a higher sperm count d. you can only fit one hand in a puppet).

Fall only for boys whose
younger sisters forgot to attend your
birthday parties.

Je Me Moi.
How to solve cases.
Paternal lectures proceed whenever
one speaks me at the beginning
of a sentence. One becomes addicted
to I just to be careful.[12]

---

12 "For the impressions that follow are no longer original. I should collect the
binding of novels of former days, but they would be the days when I read my
novels, the days my father repeated so often 'Sit up straight!' " —*Time Regained.*

v. 'signs traced through invisible ink behind her sad, submissive eyes'

The condos are coming.
If an empty lot could be declared
a heritage site. Typo, an empathy lot.
From the Regent once walking
just after a woman fell
from a fifth story window. *Warning:*
Surviving a night shift can lead
to feelings of invincibility.[13]
There is a panic of having, especially
when one drives through canyons.
Being driven, not being able
to drive, one learns
surrender. How to ask
are you speeding? without knowing
how to decipher numbers.

The upper limit of young keeps rising.
One may stop beside an aluminium
dollhouse at 16 years old and think

---

13 In the summer of 2016 I stood in a well-known West Coast Destination Bookstore, facing the Proust section. Thinking of les Demoiselles de Balbec, of Surrey Girls and all other regional variations on the mythic archetype, I was drawn to flip through an annotated edition of *In the Shadow of Young Girls in Flower*. I found the extended passage about les demoiselles, and came across a section where the narrator compares the girl on the bicycle to a *peri*. It is beyond mentioning the details one misses on first reading. Note 271 informed me that a peri—according to Persian mythology—is a supernatural being, excluded from paradise until penance is accomplished.

can I really be this young and this smart?
One will not think this twice.

There are tricks
of the middle class, tricks
of the lower and those
one swallows. Each is
an exercise in acquiring.
The first two are about mastering forms.
Tax rebates, grant proposals,
a mysterious heap of green
at the bottom of one's leatherette purse.

A vintage paperback edition
of rage and acoustics bears a rich ephemera
of late 20th century West Coast life:
a bus ticket the consistency
of rolling papers and bibles.
Past 6:30, all zones are open to one.[14]

---

14 Surrey is—for many complicated reasons—embedded in a country called
Canada, in the Greater Vancouver Regional District. Often called a bedroom
community. No one has, to my knowledge, explored the connections be-
tween this designation—the entire geography as a bedroom—and the sup-
posed loose sexual mores of the female inhabitants.

vi. "I had merely the illusion of thinking a departure'

Heart being a fail point
in a poem, substitute
a star. There is precedent.
A night in oils painted
by someone who spoke
the other language, but
shared the same country
as your grandmother. Also
translates well in one's own
phone. Also: yellow.
To say East Coast
and mean simply not here
and not prairies.[15] How to be
at a beginning
in a classroom after
almost three decades. One will be
lost and found, anachronistic,
near a phone booth. A *station-essence*,
a freeway. Embarrassed to attempt

---

15 This country has two official languages of which French is one. Official for what purpose in Surrey has never been determined. West Coast sub/urban language immersion options are limited. Grade 8 French is required. There was a mid-term. I got an A that term but resented requirements. Years later I visited France and was politely asked *parlez-vous français?* The answer—still—is *non.*

the other language, one will say
West Coast to a cab driver
and all will be forgiven. [16]

---

16 In the area of Biblical Studies, German is generally thought more useful than French. *The Dead Sea Scrolls* were discovered by French monks, however, and if you're going to read the secondary scholarship it is expected that you make an effort to master at least the ability to dissect a text of scholarship in French. I did once after spending 6 weeks in Quebec's Eastern Township, in my late 20s. To prove my competence I sat in a small basement room and translated a passage on *Le texte masorétique*. Here I learned the pronoun *On*.

vii. Vous

The diagnosis that women
remain girls for much longer.
It is acceptable especially
to uptalk, to scramble glottally.
If, in a country where the other
language dominates, one chooses
as a guide a fluent giantess from another
local sprawl who smiles too much.
In museums, one finds an interior clarion.[17]
Looking diagonally across a theatre at
a poetess can lead to vertigo.
Read at least 20 translations
per annum. Blame one's predilection
for textual three-ways and wild libraries on
childhood poverty, parenthood deprivation;
not knowing any better.
A type of information professional,
a tarot teacher does not have
to be a crone, but it helps.
One will find solace in paper

---

17 "And so what I had supposed to mean nothing to me was the only thing
in my whole life. How ignorant we are of ourselves."—*The Fugitive*. Of course
I worry about being too confessional. Because it's over done, because I'm a
girl and because do we really need another first person narrative about white
trash girls and their sweetbitter girlhoods splattered with books and moder-
ately unpleasant sexual encounters? One way to create distance in a poem is
to use *You* instead of *I*. It's a giveaway though, the *You* is almost always *I*, at
least lately.

even when it is unbound.[18]
The job of the senses is to guide.
Each image tied to an element.
Fire maps one's movement but, still, prevention
commercials one's acceptance of it. There is
an anxiety to watching it move.
One is asked for it in translated fragments,
not camping but rather handheld.

Let me check out your koi,
is something overheard
only on local buses.
One has committed
to word tattoos long
before it is trendy. The other
required language seeming
too hard, one chooses entirely
new characters. One continues
to write notes on one's hands.
Each root a triad of consonants,
decorating dots for vowels.
The dissection marks of a verb
analysis: second, feminine, plural.[19]

---

18 "She never came back ... The world is not created once and for all, for each of us individually. There are added to it, in the course of our lives, things of which we have never had any suspicion. Alas!"—*The Fugitive*. Alas, indeed.
19 Trigger warning: everyone is going to die. At a residency in Banff there is a marker of a historic house, the home of Senator Forget. Senator Forget. I mention this to other poets. They rush to correct my pronunciation: Senator *Forj-eh*. I insist: *no, no, not this time.*

The professor opens

the lecture with a grief lesson and an a-cappella requiem, as
I might have done.

She says. *On my 60th birthday, I looked in a newspaper to
discover I'd never known the word 'camouflage.'*

She says. *I dropped my doctoral program when I realized
there is more than one way, friend, to 'make knowledge.'*

She says. *Fear not! Just negotiate and don't be a girl about it.*

It's cliché but yes. We are sitting in a circle.

My classmate is blonde, rounded: kewpie doll cheekbones,
and Byzantine eyes.

A translator of vowel harmonies, a fusional agglutinative,
book language of the Northern hemisphere. Her motivating
question: *Why am I always having water dreams?*

My classmate has grey, bobbed hair, bare ankles crossed, and
I realize she's sexy: the metallic shields of her silver toenails.
Never have I seen her wearing lipstick. Her query: *Poems
always come to me when I nap? I have recently discovered my
father's notebook?*

The workshop begins by breathing together.

To the right of you is a classmate, a stranger. She asks. *My Benjamin was once Ava and I wrote her first period on a paper bag, then wondered as she was transitioning if the poem didn't want to become prose?*

> The professor instructs:
> *turn to the hollow of the page*
> *—place yourself in its centre—*
> *the mourning is a continually*
> *work-shopped poem. Write it*
> *with scissors or a pair of shears,*
> *pinking.*

Acknowledgements

The opening quotes are from Mary Ruefle, *Madness, Rack and Honey* and Timothy Lavin, "The Listener." *The Atlantic.* August, 2010.

"An epidemiology of recent muse naming patterns" was written in 2014 and was inspired in part by something said to me by Kerry Shawn Keys and by the book *Darker* by Mark Strand. "The professor opens" was inspired by things said to me by Betsy Warland, Jen Currin, Shannon Maguire, Leena Niemela, Barbara Baydala; by something overheard at a writing workshop in 2014; and by *Grief Lessons* by Anne Carson & Euripides.

"Crimes of the Century" was written while reading Jen Currin's *School* and watching the titular CNN program in Spring 2014.

"Retrospective of the North in gold" is for Dionys de Leeuw and contains a reference to Jack Gilbert.

"Crépuscule: Basic bitch variations" is for Jennifer Lapierre.

"Toronto—A New York poem" is for Ori Livneh.

For Proust quotes I relied on D.J. Enright's revised version of the translation by C.K. Moncrieff and Terence Kilmartin; and on James Grief's *In the Shadow of Young Girls in Flower.*

Both the Banff Centre for the Arts and the Canada Council funded me during the writing of this book. Earlier versions of these poems appeared in *The Rusty Toque, the Capilano Review, Arc Poetry Magazine, CV2,* and *The Malahat Review.* My thanks.

My thanks to Lisa Robertson, Karen Solie & Michael Dickman who helped with these poems at the Banff Centre in Spring 2016; Kim Trainor who helped me complete the manuscript in Vancouver's one cemetery in the Spring of 2020 and for her on-going proofreading, ordering etc.

Thanks to Anna van Valkenburg and Michael Mirolla at Guernica.

Also Omid. Also Allison, Daisy, Iris, Aimee, Aaron & Rebekka. My bubble.

About the Author

JENNIFER ZILM is the author of two previous collections: *Waiting Room* (Book*hug, 2016), which was nominated for the Robert Kroetsch Award, and *The Missing Field* (Guernica Editions, 2018), which was nominated for the Pat Lowther Award. Her poems have appeared all over the place. She is a former/failed Bible scholar, mental health worker, and a librarian/archivist. She is interested in any editing, writing, fortune telling, collage, horoscope casting, poetry reading/writing, prophesying etc. She is always on the lookout for new ways to communicate and connect and scheme. She lives in Greater Surrey Regional District and in Ecuador. Come visit her online or in-person.

MIX
Paper
FSC® C100212

Printed in June 2022
by Gauvin Press,
Gatineau, Québec